AF477195

This planner belongs to

____

____

____

____

____

____

AT A GLANCE

	JANUARY	FEBRUARY	MARCH	APRIL	MAY	JUNE
1	FRI	MON	MON	THU	SAT	TUE
2	SAT	TUE	TUE	FRI	SUN	WED
3	SUN	WED	WED	SAT	MON	THU
4	MON	THU	THU	SUN	TUE	FRI
5	TUE	FRI	FRI	MON	WED	SAT
6	WED	SAT	SAT	TUE	THU	SUN
7	THU	SUN	SUN	WED	FRI	MON
8	FRI	MON	MON	THU	SAT	TUE
9	SAT	TUE	TUE	FRI	SUN	WED
10	SUN	WED	WED	SAT	MON	THU
11	MON	THU	THU	SUN	TUE	FRI
12	TUE	FRI	FRI	MON	WED	SAT
13	WED	SAT	SAT	TUE	THU	SUN
14	THU	SUN	SUN	WED	FRI	MON
15	FRI	MON	MON	THU	SAT	TUE
16	SAT	TUE	TUE	FRI	SUN	WED
17	SUN	WED	WED	SAT	MON	THU
18	MON	THU	THU	SUN	TUE	FRI
19	TUE	FRI	FRI	MON	WED	SAT
20	WED	SAT	SAT	TUE	THU	SUN
21	THU	SUN	SUN	WED	FRI	MON
22	FRI	MON	MON	THU	SAT	TUE
23	SAT	TUE	TUE	FRI	SUN	WED
24	SUN	WED	WED	SAT	MON	THU
25	MON	THU	THU	SUN	TUE	FRI
26	TUE	FRI	FRI	MON	WED	SAT
27	WED	SAT	SAT	TUE	THU	SUN
28	THU	SUN	SUN	WED	FRI	MON
29	FRI		MON	THU	SAT	TUE
30	SAT		TUE	FRI	SUN	WED
31	SUN		WED		MON	

2021

JULY	AUGUST	SEPTEMBER	OCTOBER	NOVEMBER	DECEMBER	
THU	SUN	WED	FRI	MON	WED	1
FRI	MON	THU	SAT	TUE	THU	2
SAT	TUE	FRI	SUN	WED	FRI	3
SUN	WED	SAT	MON	THU	SAT	4
MON	THU	SUN	TUE	FRI	SUN	5
TUE	FRI	MON	WED	SAT	MON	6
WED	SAT	TUE	THU	SUN	TUE	7
THU	SUN	WED	FRI	MON	WED	8
FRI	MON	THU	SAT	TUE	THU	9
SAT	TUE	FRI	SUN	WED	FRI	10
SUN	WED	SAT	MON	THU	SAT	11
MON	THU	SUN	TUE	FRI	SUN	12
TUE	FRI	MON	WED	SAT	MON	13
WED	SAT	TUE	THU	SUN	TUE	14
THU	SUN	WED	FRI	MON	WED	15
FRI	MON	THU	SAT	TUE	THU	16
SAT	TUE	FRI	SUN	WED	FRI	17
SUN	WED	SAT	MON	THU	SAT	18
MON	THU	SUN	TUE	FRI	SUN	19
TUE	FRI	MON	WED	SAT	MON	20
WED	SAT	TUE	THU	SUN	TUE	21
THU	SUN	WED	FRI	MON	WED	22
FRI	MON	THU	SAT	TUE	THU	23
SAT	TUE	FRI	SUN	WED	FRI	24
SUN	WED	SAT	MON	THU	SAT	25
MON	THU	SUN	TUE	FRI	SUN	26
TUE	FRI	MON	WED	SAT	MON	27
WED	SAT	TUE	THU	SUN	TUE	28
THU	SUN	WED	FRI	MON	WED	29
FRI	MON	THU	SAT	TUE	THU	30
SAT	TUE		SUN		FRI	31

AT A GLANCE

	JANUARY	FEBRUARY	MARCH	APRIL	MAY	JUNE
1	SAT	TUE	TUE	FRI	SUN	WED
2	SUN	WED	WED	SAT	MON	THU
3	MON	THU	THU	SUN	TUE	FRI
4	TUE	FRI	FRI	MON	WED	SAT
5	WED	SAT	SAT	TUE	THU	SUN
6	THU	SUN	SUN	WED	FRI	MON
7	FRI	MON	MON	THU	SAT	TUE
8	SAT	TUE	TUE	FRI	SUN	WED
9	SUN	WED	WED	SAT	MON	THU
10	MON	THU	THU	SUN	TUE	FRI
11	TUE	FRI	FRI	MON	WED	SAT
12	WED	SAT	SAT	TUE	THU	SUN
13	THU	SUN	SUN	WED	FRI	MON
14	FRI	MON	MON	THU	SAT	TUE
15	SAT	TUE	TUE	FRI	SUN	WED
16	SUN	WED	WED	SAT	MON	THU
17	MON	THU	THU	SUN	TUE	FRI
18	TUE	FRI	FRI	MON	WED	SAT
19	WED	SAT	SAT	TUE	THU	SUN
20	THU	SUN	SUN	WED	FRI	MON
21	FRI	MON	MON	THU	SAT	TUE
22	SAT	TUE	TUE	FRI	SUN	WED
23	SUN	WED	WED	SAT	MON	THU
24	MON	THU	THU	SUN	TUE	FRI
25	TUE	FRI	FRI	MON	WED	SAT
26	WED	SAT	SAT	TUE	THU	SUN
27	THU	SUN	SUN	WED	FRI	MON
28	FRI	MON	MON	THU	SAT	TUE
29	SAT		TUE	FRI	SUN	WED
30	SUN		WED	SAT	MON	THU
31	MON		THU		TUE	

2022

JULY	AUGUST	SEPTEMBER	OCTOBER	NOVEMBER	DECEMBER	
FRI	MON	THU	SAT	TUE	THU	1
SAT	TUE	FRI	SUN	WED	FRI	2
SUN	WED	SAT	MON	THU	SAT	3
MON	THU	SUN	TUE	FRI	SUN	4
TUE	FRI	MON	WED	SAT	MON	5
WED	SAT	TUE	THU	SUN	TUE	6
THU	SUN	WED	FRI	MON	WED	7
FRI	MON	THU	SAT	TUE	THU	8
SAT	TUE	FRI	SUN	WED	FRI	9
SUN	WED	SAT	MON	THU	SAT	10
MON	THU	SUN	TUE	FRI	SUN	11
TUE	FRI	MON	WED	SAT	MON	12
WED	SAT	TUE	THU	SUN	TUE	13
THU	SUN	WED	FRI	MON	WED	14
FRI	MON	THU	SAT	TUE	THU	15
SAT	TUE	FRI	SUN	WED	FRI	16
SUN	WED	SAT	MON	THU	SAT	17
MON	THU	SUN	TUE	FRI	SUN	18
TUE	FRI	MON	WED	SAT	MON	19
WED	SAT	TUE	THU	SUN	TUE	20
THU	SUN	WED	FRI	MON	WED	21
FRI	MON	THU	SAT	TUE	THU	22
SAT	TUE	FRI	SUN	WED	FRI	23
SUN	WED	SAT	MON	THU	SAT	24
MON	THU	SUN	TUE	FRI	SUN	25
TUE	FRI	MON	WED	SAT	MON	26
WED	SAT	TUE	THU	SUN	TUE	27
THU	SUN	WED	FRI	MON	WED	28
FRI	MON	THU	SAT	TUE	THU	29
SAT	TUE	FRI	SUN	WED	FRI	30
SUN	WED		MON		SAT	31

28 MONDAY

7
8
9
10
11
12 PM
1
2
3
4
5
6
7
8
9

29 TUESDAY

7
8
9
10
11
12 PM
1
2
3
4
5
6
7
8
9

30 WEDNESDAY

7
8
9
10
11
12 PM
1
2
3
4
5
6
7
8
9

31 THURSDAY

7
8
9
10
11
12 PM
1
2
3
4
5
6
7
8
9

DECEMBER 2020 / JANUARY 2021

WK 53

1 FRIDAY	2 SATURDAY	3 SUNDAY
7	7	7
8	8	8
9	9	9
10	10	10
11	11	11
12 PM	12 PM	12 PM
1	1	1
2	2	2
3	3	3
4	4	4
5	5	5
6	6	6
7	7	7
8	8	8
9	9	9

Notes

To-Do

4 MONDAY	5 TUESDAY	6 WEDNESDAY	7 THURSDAY
7	7	7	7
8	8	8	8
9	9	9	9
10	10	10	10
11	11	11	11
12 PM	12 PM	12 PM	12 PM
1	1	1	1
2	2	2	2
3	3	3	3
4	4	4	4
5	5	5	5
6	6	6	6
7	7	7	7
8	8	8	8
9	9	9	9

JANUARY

WK 1

8 FRIDAY	9 SATURDAY	10 SUNDAY
7	7	7
8	8	8
9	9	9
10	10	10
11	11	11
12 PM	12 PM	12 PM
1	1	1
2	2	2
3	3	3
4	4	4
5	5	5
6	6	6
7	7	7
8	8	8
9	9	9

Notes

To-Do

- ○
- ○
- ○
- ○
- ○
- ○
- ○
- ○
- ○
- ○
- ○
- ○
- ○
- ○

11 MONDAY	12 TUESDAY	13 WEDNESDAY	14 THURSDAY
7	7	7	7
8	8	8	8
9	9	9	9
10	10	10	10
11	11	11	11
12 PM	12 PM	12 PM	12 PM
1	1	1	1
2	2	2	2
3	3	3	3
4	4	4	4
5	5	5	5
6	6	6	6
7	7	7	7
8	8	8	8
9	9	9	9

15 FRIDAY

7

8

9

10

11

12 PM

1

2

3

4

5

6

7

8

9

16 SATURDAY

7

8

9

10

11

12 PM

1

2

3

4

5

6

7

8

9

17 SUNDAY

7

8

9

10

11

12 PM

1

2

3

4

5

6

7

8

9

Notes

To-Do

- ○
- ○
- ○
- ○
- ○
- ○
- ○
- ○
- ○
- ○
- ○
- ○
- ○
- ○

18 MONDAY	19 TUESDAY	20 WEDNESDAY	21 THURSDAY
7	7	7	7
8	8	8	8
9	9	9	9
10	10	10	10
11	11	11	11
12 PM	12 PM	12 PM	12 PM
1	1	1	1
2	2	2	2
3	3	3	3
4	4	4	4
5	5	5	5
6	6	6	6
7	7	7	7
8	8	8	8
9	9	9	9

JANUARY

WK 3

22 FRIDAY	23 SATURDAY	24 SUNDAY
7	7	7
8	8	8
9	9	9
10	10	10
11	11	11
12 PM	12 PM	12 PM
1	1	1
2	2	2
3	3	3
4	4	4
5	5	5
6	6	6
7	7	7
8	8	8
9	9	9

Notes

To-Do

- ○
- ○
- ○
- ○
- ○
- ○
- ○
- ○
- ○
- ○
- ○
- ○
- ○
- ○

25 MONDAY

7

8

9

10

11

12 PM

1

2

3

4

5

6

7

8

9

26 TUESDAY

7

8

9

10

11

12 PM

1

2

3

4

5

6

7

8

9

27 WEDNESDAY

7

8

9

10

11

12 PM

1

2

3

4

5

6

7

8

9

28 THURSDAY

7

8

9

10

11

12 PM

1

2

3

4

5

6

7

8

9

JANUARY
WK 4

29 FRIDAY	30 SATURDAY	31 SUNDAY	Notes
7	7	7	
8	8	8	
9	9	9	
10	10	10	
11	11	11	
12 PM	12 PM	12 PM	
1	1	1	
2	2	2	
3	3	3	To-Do
4	4	4	○ ○
5	5	5	○ ○
6	6	6	○ ○
7	7	7	○ ○
8	8	8	○ ○
9	9	9	○ ○
			○ ○

1 MONDAY	2 TUESDAY	3 WEDNESDAY	4 THURSDAY
7	7	7	7
8	8	8	8
9	9	9	9
10	10	10	10
11	11	11	11
12 PM	12 PM	12 PM	12 PM
1	1	1	1
2	2	2	2
3	3	3	3
4	4	4	4
5	5	5	5
6	6	6	6
7	7	7	7
8	8	8	8
9	9	9	9

FEBRUARY
WK 5

5 FRIDAY	6 SATURDAY	7 SUNDAY
7	7	7
8	8	8
9	9	9
10	10	10
11	11	11
12 PM	12 PM	12 PM
1	1	1
2	2	2
3	3	3
4	4	4
5	5	5
6	6	6
7	7	7
8	8	8
9	9	9

Notes

to-Do

- ○
- ○
- ○
- ○
- ○
- ○
- ○
- ○
- ○
- ○
- ○
- ○
- ○
- ○

8 MONDAY

7
8
9
10
11
12 PM
1
2
3
4
5
6
7
8
9

9 TUESDAY

7
8
9
10
11
12 PM
1
2
3
4
5
6
7
8
9

10 WEDNESDAY

7
8
9
10
11
12 PM
1
2
3
4
5
6
7
8
9

11 THURSDAY

7
8
9
10
11
12 PM
1
2
3
4
5
6
7
8
9

FEBRUARY
WK 6

12 FRIDAY	13 SATURDAY	14 SUNDAY
7	7	7
8	8	8
9	9	9
10	10	10
11	11	11
12 PM	12 PM	12 PM
1	1	1
2	2	2
3	3	3
4	4	4
5	5	5
6	6	6
7	7	7
8	8	8
9	9	9

Notes

To-Do

- ○
- ○
- ○
- ○
- ○
- ○
- ○
- ○
- ○
- ○
- ○
- ○
- ○
- ○

15 MONDAY

7

8

9

10

11

12 PM

1

2

3

4

5

6

7

8

9

16 TUESDAY

7

8

9

10

11

12 PM

1

2

3

4

5

6

7

8

9

17 WEDNESDAY

7

8

9

10

11

12 PM

1

2

3

4

5

6

7

8

9

18 THURSDAY

7

8

9

10

11

12 PM

1

2

3

4

5

6

7

8

9

FEBRUARY

WK 7

19 FRIDAY	20 SATURDAY	21 SUNDAY
7	7	7
8	8	8
9	9	9
10	10	10
11	11	11
12 PM	12 PM	12 PM
1	1	1
2	2	2
3	3	3
4	4	4
5	5	5
6	6	6
7	7	7
8	8	8
9	9	9

Notes

To-Do

○
○
○
○
○
○
○
○
○
○
○
○
○
○

22 MONDAY	23 TUESDAY	24 WEDNESDAY	25 THURSDAY
7	7	7	7
8	8	8	8
9	9	9	9
10	10	10	10
11	11	11	11
12 PM	12 PM	12 PM	12 PM
1	1	1	1
2	2	2	2
3	3	3	3
4	4	4	4
5	5	5	5
6	6	6	6
7	7	7	7
8	8	8	8
9	9	9	9

FEBRUARY

WK 8

26 FRIDAY	27 SATURDAY	28 SUNDAY
7	7	7
8	8	8
9	9	9
10	10	10
11	11	11
12 PM	12 PM	12 PM
1	1	1
2	2	2
3	3	3
4	4	4
5	5	5
6	6	6
7	7	7
8	8	8
9	9	9

Notes

To-Do

○
○
○
○
○
○
○
○
○
○
○
○
○
○

1 MONDAY

7

8

9

10

11

12 PM

1

2

3

4

5

6

7

8

9

2 TUESDAY

7

8

9

10

11

12 PM

1

2

3

4

5

6

7

8

9

3 WEDNESDAY

7

8

9

10

11

12 PM

1

2

3

4

5

6

7

8

9

4 THURSDAY

7

8

9

10

11

12 PM

1

2

3

4

5

6

7

8

9

MARCH

WK 9

5 FRIDAY	6 SATURDAY	7 SUNDAY
7	7	7
8	8	8
9	9	9
10	10	10
11	11	11
12 PM	12 PM	12 PM
1	1	1
2	2	2
3	3	3
4	4	4
5	5	5
6	6	6
7	7	7
8	8	8
9	9	9

Notes

To-Do

- ○
- ○
- ○
- ○
- ○
- ○
- ○
- ○
- ○
- ○
- ○
- ○
- ○
- ○

8 MONDAY	9 TUESDAY	10 WEDNESDAY	11 THURSDAY
7	7	7	7
8	8	8	8
9	9	9	9
10	10	10	10
11	11	11	11
12 PM	12 PM	12 PM	12 PM
1	1	1	1
2	2	2	2
3	3	3	3
4	4	4	4
5	5	5	5
6	6	6	6
7	7	7	7
8	8	8	8
9	9	9	9

MARCH
WK 10

12 FRIDAY

13 SATURDAY

14 SUNDAY

FRIDAY	SATURDAY	SUNDAY
7	7	7
8	8	8
9	9	9
10	10	10
11	11	11
12 PM	12 PM	12 PM
1	1	1
2	2	2
3	3	3
4	4	4
5	5	5
6	6	6
7	7	7
8	8	8
9	9	9

Notes

To-Do

- ○
- ○
- ○
- ○
- ○
- ○
- ○
- ○
- ○
- ○
- ○
- ○
- ○
- ○

15 MONDAY	16 TUESDAY	17 WEDNESDAY	18 THURSDAY
7	7	7	7
8	8	8	8
9	9	9	9
10	10	10	10
11	11	11	11
12 PM	12 PM	12 PM	12 PM
1	1	1	1
2	2	2	2
3	3	3	3
4	4	4	4
5	5	5	5
6	6	6	6
7	7	7	7
8	8	8	8
9	9	9	9

19 FRIDAY	20 SATURDAY	21 SUNDAY
7	7	7
8	8	8
9	9	9
10	10	10
11	11	11
12 PM	12 PM	12 PM
1	1	1
2	2	2
3	3	3
4	4	4
5	5	5
6	6	6
7	7	7
8	8	8
9	9	9

Notes

To-Do

- ○
- ○
- ○
- ○
- ○
- ○
- ○
- ○
- ○
- ○
- ○
- ○
- ○
- ○

22 MONDAY	23 TUESDAY	24 WEDNESDAY	25 THURSDAY
7	7	7	7
8	8	8	8
9	9	9	9
10	10	10	10
11	11	11	11
12 PM	12 PM	12 PM	12 PM
1	1	1	1
2	2	2	2
3	3	3	3
4	4	4	4
5	5	5	5
6	6	6	6
7	7	7	7
8	8	8	8
9	9	9	9

MARCH
WK 12

26 FRIDAY	27 SATURDAY	28 SUNDAY
7	7	7
8	8	8
9	9	9
10	10	10
11	11	11
12 PM	12 PM	12 PM
1	1	1
2	2	2
3	3	3
4	4	4
5	5	5
6	6	6
7	7	7
8	8	8
9	9	9

Notes

To-Do

29 MONDAY

7
8
9
10
11
12 PM
1
2
3
4
5
6
7
8
9

30 TUESDAY

7
8
9
10
11
12 PM
1
2
3
4
5
6
7
8
9

31 WEDNESDAY

7
8
9
10
11
12 PM
1
2
3
4
5
6
7
8
9

1 THURSDAY

7
8
9
10
11
12 PM
1
2
3
4
5
6
7
8
9

APRIL
WK 13

2 FRIDAY	3 SATURDAY	4 SUNDAY
7	7	7
8	8	8
9	9	9
10	10	10
11	11	11
12 PM	12 PM	12 PM
1	1	1
2	2	2
3	3	3
4	4	4
5	5	5
6	6	6
7	7	7
8	8	8
9	9	9

Notes

To-Do

- ○
- ○
- ○
- ○
- ○
- ○
- ○
- ○
- ○
- ○
- ○
- ○
- ○
- ○

5 MONDAY	6 TUESDAY	7 WEDNESDAY	8 THURSDAY
7	7	7	7
8	8	8	8
9	9	9	9
10	10	10	10
11	11	11	11
12 PM	12 PM	12 PM	12 PM
1	1	1	1
2	2	2	2
3	3	3	3
4	4	4	4
5	5	5	5
6	6	6	6
7	7	7	7
8	8	8	8
9	9	9	9

APRIL
WK 14

9 FRIDAY	10 SATURDAY	11 SUNDAY
7	7	7
8	8	8
9	9	9
10	10	10
11	11	11
12 PM	12 PM	12 PM
1	1	1
2	2	2
3	3	3
4	4	4
5	5	5
6	6	6
7	7	7
8	8	8
9	9	9

Notes

To-Do

12 MONDAY	13 TUESDAY	14 WEDNESDAY	15 THURSDAY
7	7	7	7
8	8	8	8
9	9	9	9
10	10	10	10
11	11	11	11
12 PM	12 PM	12 PM	12 PM
1	1	1	1
2	2	2	2
3	3	3	3
4	4	4	4
5	5	5	5
6	6	6	6
7	7	7	7
8	8	8	8
9	9	9	9

APRIL

WK 15

16 FRIDAY	17 SATURDAY	18 SUNDAY
7	7	7
8	8	8
9	9	9
10	10	10
11	11	11
12 PM	12 PM	12 PM
1	1	1
2	2	2
3	3	3
4	4	4
5	5	5
6	6	6
7	7	7
8	8	8
9	9	9

Notes

To-Do

19 MONDAY	20 TUESDAY	21 WEDNESDAY	22 THURSDAY
7	7	7	7
8	8	8	8
9	9	9	9
10	10	10	10
11	11	11	11
12 PM	12 PM	12 PM	12 PM
1	1	1	1
2	2	2	2
3	3	3	3
4	4	4	4
5	5	5	5
6	6	6	6
7	7	7	7
8	8	8	8
9	9	9	9

APRIL

WK 16

23 FRIDAY	24 SATURDAY	25 SUNDAY
7	7	7
8	8	8
9	9	9
10	10	10
11	11	11
12 PM	12 PM	12 PM
1	1	1
2	2	2
3	3	3
4	4	4
5	5	5
6	6	6
7	7	7
8	8	8
9	9	9

Notes

To-Do

26 MONDAY

7
8
9
10
11
12 PM
1
2
3
4
5
6
7
8
9

27 TUESDAY

7
8
9
10
11
12 PM
1
2
3
4
5
6
7
8
9

28 WEDNESDAY

7
8
9
10
11
12 PM
1
2
3
4
5
6
7
8
9

29 THURSDAY

7
8
9
10
11
12 PM
1
2
3
4
5
6
7
8
9

APRIL
WK 17

30 FRIDAY	1 SATURDAY	2 SUNDAY
7	7	7
8	8	8
9	9	9
10	10	10
11	11	11
12 PM	12 PM	12 PM
1	1	1
2	2	2
3	3	3
4	4	4
5	5	5
6	6	6
7	7	7
8	8	8
9	9	9

Notes

To-Do

- ○
- ○
- ○
- ○
- ○
- ○
- ○
- ○
- ○
- ○
- ○
- ○
- ○
- ○

3 MONDAY	4 TUESDAY	5 WEDNESDAY	6 THURSDAY
7	7	7	7
8	8	8	8
9	9	9	9
10	10	10	10
11	11	11	11
12 PM	12 PM	12 PM	12 PM
1	1	1	1
2	2	2	2
3	3	3	3
4	4	4	4
5	5	5	5
6	6	6	6
7	7	7	7
8	8	8	8
9	9	9	9

MAY
WK 18

7 FRIDAY

7
8
9
10
11
12 PM
1
2
3
4
5
6
7
8
9

8 SATURDAY

7
8
9
10
11
12 PM
1
2
3
4
5
6
7
8
9

9 SUNDAY

7
8
9
10
11
12 PM
1
2
3
4
5
6
7
8
9

Notes

To-Do

- ○
- ○
- ○
- ○
- ○
- ○
- ○
- ○
- ○
- ○
- ○
- ○
- ○
- ○

10 MONDAY	11 TUESDAY	12 WEDNESDAY	13 THURSDAY
7	7	7	7
8	8	8	8
9	9	9	9
10	10	10	10
11	11	11	11
12 PM	12 PM	12 PM	12 PM
1	1	1	1
2	2	2	2
3	3	3	3
4	4	4	4
5	5	5	5
6	6	6	6
7	7	7	7
8	8	8	8
9	9	9	9

MAY
WK 19

14 FRIDAY	15 SATURDAY	16 SUNDAY
7	7	7
8	8	8
9	9	9
10	10	10
11	11	11
12 PM	12 PM	12 PM
1	1	1
2	2	2
3	3	3
4	4	4
5	5	5
6	6	6
7	7	7
8	8	8
9	9	9

Notes

To-Do

- ○
- ○
- ○
- ○
- ○
- ○
- ○
- ○
- ○
- ○
- ○
- ○
- ○
- ○

17 MONDAY	18 TUESDAY	19 WEDNESDAY	20 THURSDAY
7	7	7	7
8	8	8	8
9	9	9	9
10	10	10	10
11	11	11	11
12 PM	12 PM	12 PM	12 PM
1	1	1	1
2	2	2	2
3	3	3	3
4	4	4	4
5	5	5	5
6	6	6	6
7	7	7	7
8	8	8	8
9	9	9	9

MAY
WK 20

21 FRIDAY	22 SATURDAY	23 SUNDAY
7	7	7
8	8	8
9	9	9
10	10	10
11	11	11
12 PM	12 PM	12 PM
1	1	1
2	2	2
3	3	3
4	4	4
5	5	5
6	6	6
7	7	7
8	8	8
9	9	9

Notes

To-Do

○
○
○
○
○
○
○
○
○
○
○
○
○
○

24 MONDAY	25 TUESDAY	26 WEDNESDAY	27 THURSDAY
7	7	7	7
8	8	8	8
9	9	9	9
10	10	10	10
11	11	11	11
12 PM	12 PM	12 PM	12 PM
1	1	1	1
2	2	2	2
3	3	3	3
4	4	4	4
5	5	5	5
6	6	6	6
7	7	7	7
8	8	8	8
9	9	9	9

MAY
WK 21

28 FRIDAY	29 SATURDAY	30 SUNDAY
7	7	7
8	8	8
9	9	9
10	10	10
11	11	11
12 PM	12 PM	12 PM
1	1	1
2	2	2
3	3	3
4	4	4
5	5	5
6	6	6
7	7	7
8	8	8
9	9	9

Notes

To-Do

- ○
- ○
- ○
- ○
- ○
- ○
- ○
- ○
- ○
- ○
- ○
- ○
- ○
- ○

31 MONDAY	1 TUESDAY	2 WEDNESDAY	3 THURSDAY
7	7	7	7
8	8	8	8
9	9	9	9
10	10	10	10
11	11	11	11
12 PM	12 PM	12 PM	12 PM
1	1	1	1
2	2	2	2
3	3	3	3
4	4	4	4
5	5	5	5
6	6	6	6
7	7	7	7
8	8	8	8
9	9	9	9

JUNE
WK 22

4 FRIDAY

7
8
9
10
11
12 PM
1
2
3
4
5
6
7
8
9

5 SATURDAY

7
8
9
10
11
12 PM
1
2
3
4
5
6
7
8
9

6 SUNDAY

7
8
9
10
11
12 PM
1
2
3
4
5
6
7
8
9

Notes

To-Do

- ○
- ○
- ○
- ○
- ○
- ○
- ○
- ○
- ○
- ○
- ○
- ○
- ○
- ○

7 MONDAY	8 TUESDAY	9 WEDNESDAY	10 THURSDAY
7	7	7	7
8	8	8	8
9	9	9	9
10	10	10	10
11	11	11	11
12 PM	12 PM	12 PM	12 PM
1	1	1	1
2	2	2	2
3	3	3	3
4	4	4	4
5	5	5	5
6	6	6	6
7	7	7	7
8	8	8	8
9	9	9	9

JUNE
WK 23

11 FRIDAY

7
8
9
10
11
12 PM
1
2
3
4
5
6
7
8
9

12 SATURDAY

7
8
9
10
11
12 PM
1
2
3
4
5
6
7
8
9

13 SUNDAY

7
8
9
10
11
12 PM
1
2
3
4
5
6
7
8
9

Notes

To-Do

14 MONDAY	15 TUESDAY	16 WEDNESDAY	17 THURSDAY
7	7	7	7
8	8	8	8
9	9	9	9
10	10	10	10
11	11	11	11
12 PM	12 PM	12 PM	12 PM
1	1	1	1
2	2	2	2
3	3	3	3
4	4	4	4
5	5	5	5
6	6	6	6
7	7	7	7
8	8	8	8
9	9	9	9

JUNE
WK 24

18 FRIDAY	19 SATURDAY	20 SUNDAY
7	7	7
8	8	8
9	9	9
10	10	10
11	11	11
12 PM	12 PM	12 PM
1	1	1
2	2	2
3	3	3
4	4	4
5	5	5
6	6	6
7	7	7
8	8	8
9	9	9

Notes

To-Do

- ○
- ○
- ○
- ○
- ○
- ○
- ○
- ○
- ○
- ○
- ○
- ○
- ○
- ○

21 MONDAY

7

8

9

10

11

12 PM

1

2

3

4

5

6

7

8

9

22 TUESDAY

7

8

9

10

11

12 PM

1

2

3

4

5

6

7

8

9

23 WEDNESDAY

7

8

9

10

11

12 PM

1

2

3

4

5

6

7

8

9

24 THURSDAY

7

8

9

10

11

12 PM

1

2

3

4

5

6

7

8

9

25 FRIDAY	26 SATURDAY	27 SUNDAY
7	7	7
8	8	8
9	9	9
10	10	10
11	11	11
12 PM	12 PM	12 PM
1	1	1
2	2	2
3	3	3
4	4	4
5	5	5
6	6	6
7	7	7
8	8	8
9	9	9

Notes

To-Do

28 MONDAY	29 TUESDAY	30 WEDNESDAY	1 THURSDAY
7	7	7	7
8	8	8	8
9	9	9	9
10	10	10	10
11	11	11	11
12 PM	12 PM	12 PM	12 PM
1	1	1	1
2	2	2	2
3	3	3	3
4	4	4	4
5	5	5	5
6	6	6	6
7	7	7	7
8	8	8	8
9	9	9	9

JULY

WK 26

2 FRIDAY	3 SATURDAY	4 SUNDAY
7	7	7
8	8	8
9	9	9
10	10	10
11	11	11
12 PM	12 PM	12 PM
1	1	1
2	2	2
3	3	3
4	4	4
5	5	5
6	6	6
7	7	7
8	8	8
9	9	9

Notes

To-Do

- ○
- ○
- ○
- ○
- ○
- ○
- ○
- ○
- ○
- ○
- ○
- ○
- ○
- ○

5 MONDAY	6 TUESDAY	7 WEDNESDAY	8 THURSDAY
7	7	7	7
8	8	8	8
9	9	9	9
10	10	10	10
11	11	11	11
12 PM	12 PM	12 PM	12 PM
1	1	1	1
2	2	2	2
3	3	3	3
4	4	4	4
5	5	5	5
6	6	6	6
7	7	7	7
8	8	8	8
9	9	9	9

JULY
WK 27

9 FRIDAY	10 SATURDAY	11 SUNDAY
7	7	7
8	8	8
9	9	9
10	10	10
11	11	11
12 PM	12 PM	12 PM
1	1	1
2	2	2
3	3	3
4	4	4
5	5	5
6	6	6
7	7	7
8	8	8
9	9	9

Notes

To-Do

- ○
- ○
- ○
- ○
- ○
- ○
- ○
- ○
- ○
- ○
- ○
- ○
- ○
- ○

12 MONDAY	13 TUESDAY	14 WEDNESDAY	15 THURSDAY
7	7	7	7
8	8	8	8
9	9	9	9
10	10	10	10
11	11	11	11
12 PM	12 PM	12 PM	12 PM
1	1	1	1
2	2	2	2
3	3	3	3
4	4	4	4
5	5	5	5
6	6	6	6
7	7	7	7
8	8	8	8
9	9	9	9

JULY

WK 28

16 FRIDAY

7
8
9
10
11
12 PM
1
2
3
4
5
6
7
8
9

17 SATURDAY

7
8
9
10
11
12 PM
1
2
3
4
5
6
7
8
9

18 SUNDAY

7
8
9
10
11
12 PM
1
2
3
4
5
6
7
8
9

Notes

To-Do

○
○
○
○
○
○
○
○
○
○
○
○
○
○

19 MONDAY	20 TUESDAY	21 WEDNESDAY	22 THURSDAY
7	7	7	7
8	8	8	8
9	9	9	9
10	10	10	10
11	11	11	11
12 PM	12 PM	12 PM	12 PM
1	1	1	1
2	2	2	2
3	3	3	3
4	4	4	4
5	5	5	5
6	6	6	6
7	7	7	7
8	8	8	8
9	9	9	9

JULY
WK 29

23 FRIDAY	24 SATURDAY	25 SUNDAY
7	7	7
8	8	8
9	9	9
10	10	10
11	11	11
12 PM	12 PM	12 PM
1	1	1
2	2	2
3	3	3
4	4	4
5	5	5
6	6	6
7	7	7
8	8	8
9	9	9

Notes

To-Do

- ○
- ○
- ○
- ○
- ○
- ○
- ○
- ○
- ○
- ○
- ○
- ○
- ○
- ○

26 MONDAY	27 TUESDAY	28 WEDNESDAY	29 THURSDAY
7	7	7	7
8	8	8	8
9	9	9	9
10	10	10	10
11	11	11	11
12 PM	12 PM	12 PM	12 PM
1	1	1	1
2	2	2	2
3	3	3	3
4	4	4	4
5	5	5	5
6	6	6	6
7	7	7	7
8	8	8	8
9	9	9	9

JULY
WK 30

30 FRIDAY

7
8
9
10
11
12 PM
1
2
3
4
5
6
7
8
9

31 SATURDAY

7
8
9
10
11
12 PM
1
2
3
4
5
6
7
8
9

1 SUNDAY

7
8
9
10
11
12 PM
1
2
3
4
5
6
7
8
9

Notes

To-Do

- ○
- ○
- ○
- ○
- ○
- ○
- ○
- ○
- ○
- ○
- ○
- ○
- ○
- ○

2 MONDAY	3 TUESDAY	4 WEDNESDAY	5 THURSDAY
7	7	7	7
8	8	8	8
9	9	9	9
10	10	10	10
11	11	11	11
12 PM	12 PM	12 PM	12 PM
1	1	1	1
2	2	2	2
3	3	3	3
4	4	4	4
5	5	5	5
6	6	6	6
7	7	7	7
8	8	8	8
9	9	9	9

AUGUST

WK 31

6 FRIDAY	7 SATURDAY	8 SUNDAY
7	7	7
8	8	8
9	9	9
10	10	10
11	11	11
12 PM	12 PM	12 PM
1	1	1
2	2	2
3	3	3
4	4	4
5	5	5
6	6	6
7	7	7
8	8	8
9	9	9

Notes

To-Do

- ○
- ○
- ○
- ○
- ○
- ○
- ○
- ○
- ○
- ○
- ○
- ○
- ○
- ○

9 MONDAY	10 TUESDAY	11 WEDNESDAY	12 THURSDAY
7	7	7	7
8	8	8	8
9	9	9	9
10	10	10	10
11	11	11	11
12 PM	12 PM	12 PM	12 PM
1	1	1	1
2	2	2	2
3	3	3	3
4	4	4	4
5	5	5	5
6	6	6	6
7	7	7	7
8	8	8	8
9	9	9	9

AUGUST
WK 32

13 FRIDAY	14 SATURDAY	15 SUNDAY	Notes
7	7	7	
8	8	8	
9	9	9	
10	10	10	
11	11	11	
12 PM	12 PM	12 PM	
1	1	1	
2	2	2	
3	3	3	To-Do
4	4	4	○
			○
5	5	5	○
			○
6	6	6	○
			○
7	7	7	○
			○
8	8	8	○
			○
9	9	9	○
			○
			○
			○

16 MONDAY

7
8
9
10
11
12 PM
1
2
3
4
5
6
7
8
9

17 TUESDAY

7
8
9
10
11
12 PM
1
2
3
4
5
6
7
8
9

18 WEDNESDAY

7
8
9
10
11
12 PM
1
2
3
4
5
6
7
8
9

19 THURSDAY

7
8
9
10
11
12 PM
1
2
3
4
5
6
7
8
9

AUGUST
WK 33

20 FRIDAY

7
8
9
10
11
12 PM
1
2
3
4
5
6
7
8
9

21 SATURDAY

7
8
9
10
11
12 PM
1
2
3
4
5
6
7
8
9

22 SUNDAY

7
8
9
10
11
12 PM
1
2
3
4
5
6
7
8
9

Notes

To-Do

23 MONDAY

7
8
9
10
11
12 PM
1
2
3
4
5
6
7
8
9

24 TUESDAY

7
8
9
10
11
12 PM
1
2
3
4
5
6
7
8
9

25 WEDNESDAY

7
8
9
10
11
12 PM
1
2
3
4
5
6
7
8
9

26 THURSDAY

7
8
9
10
11
12 PM
1
2
3
4
5
6
7
8
9

AUGUST
WK 34

27 FRIDAY	28 SATURDAY	29 SUNDAY
7	7	7
8	8	8
9	9	9
10	10	10
11	11	11
12 PM	12 PM	12 PM
1	1	1
2	2	2
3	3	3
4	4	4
5	5	5
6	6	6
7	7	7
8	8	8
9	9	9

Notes

To-Do

- ○
- ○
- ○
- ○
- ○
- ○
- ○
- ○
- ○
- ○
- ○
- ○
- ○
- ○

30 MONDAY	31 TUESDAY	1 WEDNESDAY	2 THURSDAY
7	7	7	7
8	8	8	8
9	9	9	9
10	10	10	10
11	11	11	11
12 PM	12 PM	12 PM	12 PM
1	1	1	1
2	2	2	2
3	3	3	3
4	4	4	4
5	5	5	5
6	6	6	6
7	7	7	7
8	8	8	8
9	9	9	9

SEPTEMBER
WK 35

3 FRIDAY	4 SATURDAY	5 SUNDAY	Notes
7	7	7	
8	8	8	
9	9	9	
10	10	10	
11	11	11	
12 PM	12 PM	12 PM	
1	1	1	
2	2	2	
3	3	3	To-Do
4	4	4	○
			○
5	5	5	○
			○
6	6	6	○
			○
7	7	7	○
			○
8	8	8	○
			○
9	9	9	○
			○
			○
			○

6 MONDAY	7 TUESDAY	8 WEDNESDAY	9 THURSDAY
7	7	7	7
8	8	8	8
9	9	9	9
10	10	10	10
11	11	11	11
12 PM	12 PM	12 PM	12 PM
1	1	1	1
2	2	2	2
3	3	3	3
4	4	4	4
5	5	5	5
6	6	6	6
7	7	7	7
8	8	8	8
9	9	9	9

SEPTEMBER
WK 36

10 FRIDAY	11 SATURDAY	12 SUNDAY
7	7	7
8	8	8
9	9	9
10	10	10
11	11	11
12 PM	12 PM	12 PM
1	1	1
2	2	2
3	3	3
4	4	4
5	5	5
6	6	6
7	7	7
8	8	8
9	9	9

Notes

To-Do

○
○
○
○
○
○
○
○
○
○
○
○
○
○

13 MONDAY	14 TUESDAY	15 WEDNESDAY	16 THURSDAY
7	7	7	7
8	8	8	8
9	9	9	9
10	10	10	10
11	11	11	11
12 PM	12 PM	12 PM	12 PM
1	1	1	1
2	2	2	2
3	3	3	3
4	4	4	4
5	5	5	5
6	6	6	6
7	7	7	7
8	8	8	8
9	9	9	9

SEPTEMBER

WK 37

17 FRIDAY	18 SATURDAY	19 SUNDAY
7	7	7
8	8	8
9	9	9
10	10	10
11	11	11
12 PM	12 PM	12 PM
1	1	1
2	2	2
3	3	3
4	4	4
5	5	5
6	6	6
7	7	7
8	8	8
9	9	9

Notes

To-Do

- ○
- ○
- ○
- ○
- ○
- ○
- ○
- ○
- ○
- ○
- ○
- ○
- ○
- ○

20 MONDAY	21 TUESDAY	22 WEDNESDAY	23 THURSDAY
7	7	7	7
8	8	8	8
9	9	9	9
10	10	10	10
11	11	11	11
12 PM	12 PM	12 PM	12 PM
1	1	1	1
2	2	2	2
3	3	3	3
4	4	4	4
5	5	5	5
6	6	6	6
7	7	7	7
8	8	8	8
9	9	9	9

SEPTEMBER
WK 38

24 FRIDAY

7
8
9
10
11
12 PM
1
2
3
4
5
6
7
8
9

25 SATURDAY

7
8
9
10
11
12 PM
1
2
3
4
5
6
7
8
9

26 SUNDAY

7
8
9
10
11
12 PM
1
2
3
4
5
6
7
8
9

Notes

To-Do

○
○
○
○
○
○
○
○
○
○
○
○
○
○

27 MONDAY	28 TUESDAY	29 WEDNESDAY	30 THURSDAY
7	7	7	7
8	8	8	8
9	9	9	9
10	10	10	10
11	11	11	11
12 PM	12 PM	12 PM	12 PM
1	1	1	1
2	2	2	2
3	3	3	3
4	4	4	4
5	5	5	5
6	6	6	6
7	7	7	7
8	8	8	8
9	9	9	9

OCTOBER
WK 39

1 FRIDAY	2 SATURDAY	3 SUNDAY
7	7	7
8	8	8
9	9	9
10	10	10
11	11	11
12 PM	12 PM	12 PM
1	1	1
2	2	2
3	3	3
4	4	4
5	5	5
6	6	6
7	7	7
8	8	8
9	9	9

Notes

To-Do

- ○
- ○
- ○
- ○
- ○
- ○
- ○
- ○
- ○
- ○
- ○
- ○
- ○
- ○

4 MONDAY	5 TUESDAY	6 WEDNESDAY	7 THURSDAY
7	7	7	7
8	8	8	8
9	9	9	9
10	10	10	10
11	11	11	11
12 PM	12 PM	12 PM	12 PM
1	1	1	1
2	2	2	2
3	3	3	3
4	4	4	4
5	5	5	5
6	6	6	6
7	7	7	7
8	8	8	8
9	9	9	9

OCTOBER
WK 40

8 FRIDAY	9 SATURDAY	10 SUNDAY	Notes
7	7	7	
8	8	8	
9	9	9	
10	10	10	
11	11	11	
12 PM	12 PM	12 PM	
1	1	1	
2	2	2	
3	3	3	To-Do
4	4	4	○
5	5	5	○
6	6	6	○
7	7	7	○
8	8	8	○
9	9	9	○

11 MONDAY	12 TUESDAY	13 WEDNESDAY	14 THURSDAY
7	7	7	7
8	8	8	8
9	9	9	9
10	10	10	10
11	11	11	11
12 PM	12 PM	12 PM	12 PM
1	1	1	1
2	2	2	2
3	3	3	3
4	4	4	4
5	5	5	5
6	6	6	6
7	7	7	7
8	8	8	8
9	9	9	9

OCTOBER
WK 41

15 FRIDAY

7
8
9
10
11
12 PM
1
2
3
4
5
6
7
8
9

16 SATURDAY

7
8
9
10
11
12 PM
1
2
3
4
5
6
7
8
9

17 SUNDAY

7
8
9
10
11
12 PM
1
2
3
4
5
6
7
8
9

Notes

To-Do

○
○
○
○
○
○
○
○
○
○
○
○
○
○

18 MONDAY	19 TUESDAY	20 WEDNESDAY	21 THURSDAY
7	7	7	7
8	8	8	8
9	9	9	9
10	10	10	10
11	11	11	11
12 PM	12 PM	12 PM	12 PM
1	1	1	1
2	2	2	2
3	3	3	3
4	4	4	4
5	5	5	5
6	6	6	6
7	7	7	7
8	8	8	8
9	9	9	9

OCTOBER

WK 42

22 FRIDAY

7
8
9
10
11
12 PM
1
2
3
4
5
6
7
8
9

23 SATURDAY

7
8
9
10
11
12 PM
1
2
3
4
5
6
7
8
9

24 SUNDAY

7
8
9
10
11
12 PM
1
2
3
4
5
6
7
8
9

Notes

To-Do

25 MONDAY

7

8

9

10

11

12 PM

1

2

3

4

5

6

7

8

9

26 TUESDAY

7

8

9

10

11

12 PM

1

2

3

4

5

6

7

8

9

27 WEDNESDAY

7

8

9

10

11

12 PM

1

2

3

4

5

6

7

8

9

28 THURSDAY

7

8

9

10

11

12 PM

1

2

3

4

5

6

7

8

9

OCTOBER
WK 43

29 FRIDAY

7
8
9
10
11
12 PM
1
2
3
4
5
6
7
8
9

30 SATURDAY

7
8
9
10
11
12 PM
1
2
3
4
5
6
7
8
9

31 SUNDAY

7
8
9
10
11
12 PM
1
2
3
4
5
6
7
8
9

Notes

To-Do

1 MONDAY	2 TUESDAY	3 WEDNESDAY	4 THURSDAY
7	7	7	7
8	8	8	8
9	9	9	9
10	10	10	10
11	11	11	11
12 PM	12 PM	12 PM	12 PM
1	1	1	1
2	2	2	2
3	3	3	3
4	4	4	4
5	5	5	5
6	6	6	6
7	7	7	7
8	8	8	8
9	9	9	9

NOVEMBER

WK 44

5 FRIDAY

7

8

9

10

11

12 PM

1

2

3

4

5

6

7

8

9

6 SATURDAY

7

8

9

10

11

12 PM

1

2

3

4

5

6

7

8

9

7 SUNDAY

7

8

9

10

11

12 PM

1

2

3

4

5

6

7

8

9

Notes

To-Do

- ○
- ○
- ○
- ○
- ○
- ○
- ○
- ○
- ○
- ○
- ○
- ○
- ○
- ○

8 MONDAY	9 TUESDAY	10 WEDNESDAY	11 THURSDAY
7	7	7	7
8	8	8	8
9	9	9	9
10	10	10	10
11	11	11	11
12 PM	12 PM	12 PM	12 PM
1	1	1	1
2	2	2	2
3	3	3	3
4	4	4	4
5	5	5	5
6	6	6	6
7	7	7	7
8	8	8	8
9	9	9	9

NOVEMBER
WK 45

12 FRIDAY	13 SATURDAY	14 SUNDAY
7	7	7
8	8	8
9	9	9
10	10	10
11	11	11
12 PM	12 PM	12 PM
1	1	1
2	2	2
3	3	3
4	4	4
5	5	5
6	6	6
7	7	7
8	8	8
9	9	9

Notes

To-Do

- ○
- ○
- ○
- ○
- ○
- ○
- ○
- ○
- ○
- ○
- ○
- ○
- ○
- ○

15 MONDAY	16 TUESDAY	17 WEDNESDAY	18 THURSDAY
7	7	7	7
8	8	8	8
9	9	9	9
10	10	10	10
11	11	11	11
12 PM	12 PM	12 PM	12 PM
1	1	1	1
2	2	2	2
3	3	3	3
4	4	4	4
5	5	5	5
6	6	6	6
7	7	7	7
8	8	8	8
9	9	9	9

NOVEMBER
WK 46

19 FRIDAY	20 SATURDAY	21 SUNDAY
7	7	7
8	8	8
9	9	9
10	10	10
11	11	11
12 PM	12 PM	12 PM
1	1	1
2	2	2
3	3	3
4	4	4
5	5	5
6	6	6
7	7	7
8	8	8
9	9	9

Notes

To-Do

- ○
- ○
- ○
- ○
- ○
- ○
- ○
- ○
- ○
- ○
- ○
- ○
- ○
- ○

22 MONDAY

7

8

9

10

11

12 PM

1

2

3

4

5

6

7

8

9

23 TUESDAY

7

8

9

10

11

12 PM

1

2

3

4

5

6

7

8

9

24 WEDNESDAY

7

8

9

10

11

12 PM

1

2

3

4

5

6

7

8

9

25 THURSDAY

7

8

9

10

11

12 PM

1

2

3

4

5

6

7

8

9

NOVEMBER
WK 47

26 FRIDAY	27 SATURDAY	28 SUNDAY
7	7	7
8	8	8
9	9	9
10	10	10
11	11	11
12 PM	12 PM	12 PM
1	1	1
2	2	2
3	3	3
4	4	4
5	5	5
6	6	6
7	7	7
8	8	8
9	9	9

Notes

To-Do

- ○
- ○
- ○
- ○
- ○
- ○
- ○
- ○
- ○
- ○
- ○
- ○
- ○
- ○

29 MONDAY	30 TUESDAY	1 WEDNESDAY	2 THURSDAY
7	7	7	7
8	8	8	8
9	9	9	9
10	10	10	10
11	11	11	11
12 PM	12 PM	12 PM	12 PM
1	1	1	1
2	2	2	2
3	3	3	3
4	4	4	4
5	5	5	5
6	6	6	6
7	7	7	7
8	8	8	8
9	9	9	9

DECEMBER

WK 48

3 FRIDAY

4 SATURDAY

5 SUNDAY

3 FRIDAY	4 SATURDAY	5 SUNDAY
7	7	7
8	8	8
9	9	9
10	10	10
11	11	11
12 PM	12 PM	12 PM
1	1	1
2	2	2
3	3	3
4	4	4
5	5	5
6	6	6
7	7	7
8	8	8
9	9	9

Notes

To-Do

- ○
- ○
- ○
- ○
- ○
- ○
- ○
- ○
- ○
- ○
- ○
- ○
- ○
- ○

6 MONDAY	7 TUESDAY	8 WEDNESDAY	9 THURSDAY
7	7	7	7
8	8	8	8
9	9	9	9
10	10	10	10
11	11	11	11
12 PM	12 PM	12 PM	12 PM
1	1	1	1
2	2	2	2
3	3	3	3
4	4	4	4
5	5	5	5
6	6	6	6
7	7	7	7
8	8	8	8
9	9	9	9

DECEMBER

WK 49

10 FRIDAY

7
8
9
10
11
12 PM
1
2
3
4
5
6
7
8
9

11 SATURDAY

7
8
9
10
11
12 PM
1
2
3
4
5
6
7
8
9

12 SUNDAY

7
8
9
10
11
12 PM
1
2
3
4
5
6
7
8
9

Notes

To-Do

- ○
- ○
- ○
- ○
- ○
- ○
- ○
- ○
- ○
- ○
- ○
- ○
- ○
- ○

13 MONDAY

7
8
9
10
11
12 PM
1
2
3
4
5
6
7
8
9

14 TUESDAY

7
8
9
10
11
12 PM
1
2
3
4
5
6
7
8
9

15 WEDNESDAY

7
8
9
10
11
12 PM
1
2
3
4
5
6
7
8
9

16 THURSDAY

7
8
9
10
11
12 PM
1
2
3
4
5
6
7
8
9

DECEMBER
WK 50

17 FRIDAY

7
8
9
10
11
12 PM
1
2
3
4
5
6
7
8
9

18 SATURDAY

7
8
9
10
11
12 PM
1
2
3
4
5
6
7
8
9

19 SUNDAY

7
8
9
10
11
12 PM
1
2
3
4
5
6
7
8
9

Notes

To-Do

- ○
- ○
- ○
- ○
- ○
- ○
- ○
- ○
- ○
- ○
- ○
- ○
- ○
- ○

20 MONDAY	21 TUESDAY	22 WEDNESDAY	23 THURSDAY
7	7	7	7
8	8	8	8
9	9	9	9
10	10	10	10
11	11	11	11
12 PM	12 PM	12 PM	12 PM
1	1	1	1
2	2	2	2
3	3	3	3
4	4	4	4
5	5	5	5
6	6	6	6
7	7	7	7
8	8	8	8
9	9	9	9

DECEMBER
WK 51

24 FRIDAY	25 SATURDAY	26 SUNDAY
7	7	7
8	8	8
9	9	9
10	10	10
11	11	11
12 PM	12 PM	12 PM
1	1	1
2	2	2
3	3	3
4	4	4
5	5	5
6	6	6
7	7	7
8	8	8
9	9	9

Notes

To-Do

- ○
- ○
- ○
- ○
- ○
- ○
- ○
- ○
- ○
- ○
- ○
- ○
- ○
- ○

27 MONDAY	28 TUESDAY	29 WEDNESDAY	30 THURSDAY
7	7	7	7
8	8	8	8
9	9	9	9
10	10	10	10
11	11	11	11
12 PM	12 PM	12 PM	12 PM
1	1	1	1
2	2	2	2
3	3	3	3
4	4	4	4
5	5	5	5
6	6	6	6
7	7	7	7
8	8	8	8
9	9	9	9

DECEMBER
WK 52

31 FRIDAY	1 SATURDAY	2 SUNDAY	Notes
7	7	7	
8	8	8	
9	9	9	
10	10	10	
11	11	11	
12 PM	12 PM	12 PM	
1	1	1	
2	2	2	
3	3	3	To-Do
4	4	4	○
5	5	5	○
6	6	6	○
7	7	7	○
8	8	8	○
9	9	9	○

MONDAY	TUESDAY	WEDNESDAY	THURSDAY
28	29	30	31
4	5	6	7
11	12	13	14
18	19	20	21
25	26	27	28

JANUARY

FRIDAY	SATURDAY	SUNDAY
1	2	3
8	9	10
15	16	17
22	23	24
29	30	31

MONDAY	TUESDAY	WEDNESDAY	THURSDAY
1	2	3	4
8	9	10	11
15	16	17	18
22	23	24	25
1	2	3	4

FEBRUARY

FRIDAY	SATURDAY	SUNDAY
5	6	7
12	13	14
19	20	21
26	27	28
5	6	7

MONDAY	TUESDAY	WEDNESDAY	THURSDAY
1	2	3	4
8	9	10	11
15	16	17	18
22	23	24	25
29	30	31	1

MARCH

FRIDAY	SATURDAY	SUNDAY
5	6	7
12	13	14
19	20	21
26	27	28
2	3	4

MONDAY	TUESDAY	WEDNESDAY	THURSDAY
29	30	31	1
5	6	7	8
12	13	14	15
19	20	21	22
26	27	28	29

APRIL

FRIDAY	SATURDAY	SUNDAY
2	3	4
9	10	11
16	17	18
23	24	25
30	1	2

MONDAY	TUESDAY	WEDNESDAY	THURSDAY
26	27	28	29
3	4	5	6
10	11	12	13
17	18	19	20
24 / 31	25	26	27

MAY

FRIDAY	SATURDAY	SUNDAY
30	1	2
7	8	9
14	15	16
21	22	23
28	29	30

MONDAY	TUESDAY	WEDNESDAY	THURSDAY
31	1	2	3
7	8	9	10
14	15	16	17
21	22	23	24
28	29	30	1

JUNE

FRIDAY	SATURDAY	SUNDAY
4	5	6
11	12	13
18	19	20
25	26	27
2	3	4

MONDAY	TUESDAY	WEDNESDAY	THURSDAY
28	29	30	1
5	6	7	8
12	13	14	15
19	20	21	22
26	27	28	29

JULY

FRIDAY	SATURDAY	SUNDAY
2	3	4
9	10	11
16	17	18
23	24	25
30	31	1

MONDAY	TUESDAY	WEDNESDAY	THURSDAY
26	27	28	29
2	3	4	5
9	10	11	12
16	17	18	19
23 / 30	24 / 31	25	26

AUGUST

FRIDAY	SATURDAY	SUNDAY
30	31	1
6	7	8
13	14	15
20	21	22
27	28	29

MONDAY	TUESDAY	WEDNESDAY	THURSDAY
30	31	1	2
6	7	8	9
13	14	15	16
20	21	22	23
27	28	29	30

SEPTEMBER

FRIDAY	SATURDAY	SUNDAY
3	4	5
10	11	12
17	18	19
24	25	26
1	2	3

MONDAY	TUESDAY	WEDNESDAY	THURSDAY
27	28	29	30
4	5	6	7
11	12	13	14
18	19	20	21
25	26	27	28

OCTOBER

FRIDAY	SATURDAY	SUNDAY
1	2	3
8	9	10
15	16	17
22	23	24
29	30	31

MONDAY	TUESDAY	WEDNESDAY	THURSDAY
1	2	3	4
8	9	10	11
15	16	17	18
22	23	24	25
29	30	1	2

NOVEMBER

FRIDAY	SATURDAY	SUNDAY
5	6	7
12	13	14
19	20	21
26	27	28
3	4	5

MONDAY	TUESDAY	WEDNESDAY	THURSDAY
29	30	1	2
6	7	8	9
13	14	15	16
20	21	22	23
27	28	29	30

DECEMBER

FRIDAY	SATURDAY	SUNDAY
3	4	5
10	11	12
17	18	19
24	25	26
31	1	2

	MON	TUE	WED	THU	FRI	SAT	SUN

WEEKLY SCHEDULE

🕘	MON	TUE	WED	THU	FRI	SAT	SUN

Date:	Subject:
Participants:	

Notes

Date:	Subject:
Participants:	

Notes

MEETING NOTES

Date:	Subject:
Participants:	

Notes

Date:	Subject:
Participants:	

Notes

Date:	Subject:
Participants:	

Notes

Date:	Subject:
Participants:	

Notes

MEETING NOTES

Date:	Subject:
Participants:	

Notes

Date:	Subject:
Participants:	

Notes

Date:	Subject:
Participants:	

Notes

Date:	Subject:
Participants:	

Notes

MEETING NOTES

Date:	Subject:
Participants:	

Notes

Date:	Subject:
Participants:	

Notes

Date:	Subject:
Participants:	

Notes

Date:	Subject:
Participants:	

Notes

MEETING NOTES

Date:	Subject:
Participants:	

Notes

Date:	Subject:
Participants:	

Notes

	Date	Description of Expense	Category	Amount	Payment Type
1					
2					
3					
4					
5					
6					
7					
8					
9					
10					
11					
12					
13					
14					
15					
16					
17					
18					
19					
20					
21					
22					
23					
24					
25					
26					
27					
28					
29					
30					

EXPENSE TRACKER

	Date	Description of Expense	Category	Amount	Payment Type
31					
32					
33					
34					
35					
36					
37					
38					
39					
40					
41					
42					
43					
44					
45					
46					
47					
48					
49					
50					
51					
52					
53					
54					
55					
56					
57					
58					
59					
60					

	Date	Description of Expense	Category	Amount	Payment Type
61					
62					
63					
64					
65					
66					
67					
68					
69					
70					
71					
72					
73					
74					
75					
76					
77					
78					
79					
80					
81					
82					
83					
84					
85					
86					
87					
88					
89					
90					

EXPENSE TRACKER

	Date	Description of Expense	Category	Amount	Payment Type
91					
92					
93					
94					
95					
96					
97					
98					
99					
100					
101					
102					
103					
104					
105					
106					
107					
108					
109					
110					
111					
112					
113					
114					
115					
116					
117					
118					
119					
120					

NOTES

NOTES

NOTES

NOTES

CONTACTS

CONTACTS

www.ingramcontent.com/pod-product-compliance
Lightning Source LLC
LaVergne TN
LVHW081718210726
843527LV00006B/329